THE LIFE STORY OF GIPSY CORNELIUS SMITH.

THE LIFE STORY

OF

GIPSY

CORNELIUS SMITH.

JOHN HEYWOOD,
DEANSGATE AND RIDGEFIELD, MANCHESTER;
1, PATERNOSTER BUILDINGS,
LONDON.

PREFACE.

I HAVE frequently been asked by many friends to give some account, in book form, of God's dealings with me. I do so after much prayer, trusting that, as these pages are read, many may be led to magnify the grace of God, and consecrate all their powers to the service of Jesus Christ.

CORNELIUS SMITH.

Sedgwick Street, Mill Road,
Cambridge.

CONTENTS.

THE LIFE STORY OF GIPSY CORNELIUS SMITH.

CHAPTER I.

EARLY DAYS.

I CORNELIUS SMITH was born in a gipsy's tent, on May the 8th, 1831, in the parish of Burwell, Cambridgeshire, in a country lane known as Burwell Nest. My father and mother, James and Elizabeth Smith, were married at Longstanton, Cambridgeshire, their occupation being chair caners and basket makers. It was their custom to travel from place to place; thus rambling to fairs, feasts, and races, I was dragged up in darkness, misery, and sin, and became very daring and wicked, and loved the roaming life intensely. My father was a drunkard, and when he drank and smoked

I tried to imitate him, and eventually succeeded. When quite a boy an elder brother taught me to play the violin. Being passionately fond of music (which is characteristic of the gipsy race), I soon became an accomplished player, and was sought for on every hand. This led me intc further worldliness and sin.

About this time my brother went to Romford market, Essex, to buy a horse, and on returning home he was seized with sudden illness. The doctor was sent for, and on his arrival said there was no hope for him. My mother being a moral woman never would (though a gipsy) allow us to go to bed without saying the Lord's Prayer. I shall never forget the scene around the bed in that gipsy tent in Fairlop Forest, near Chigwell Row. My mother said to my brother, "Do you think about the Lord, my dear?" He looked up and said, "Yes; that is all my study." On Friday there was a very great change in him—the pain had ceased, and mortification set in on Saturday morning. We were all called to his bedside, when he stretched out his hands and said "Good-bye" three times; "I am not afraid to die," and so passed away. He was a loving son and brother, and left a void in our gipsy home that nothin seemed to fill up. My father rushed to drink to drown his sorrow. Had he known the plan of salvation, and God's love to poor troubled souls, he would have taken his burden to Him.

One night, my father, coming home the worse for drink, sitting on the front of his van, fell off, and both wheels passed over his body. He was brought home, and we thought he would die. I have since thought that God allowed this to happen to work out His own purposes. My father was so very ill that he wished my mother to take a cottage in Cambridge that he might go to the hospital. She did so, and he was somewhat restored, but through this accident was a sufferer for life.

As far as I can remember, I was then about ten years of age, and having been brought up in lanes and wayside roads, coming to a town to live in a cottage was quite a new life to me. I eagerly watched the boys with their slates round their necks and their dinner bags over their shoulders, and wondered where they were going. I followed them, until I found myself at the ragged school. For some time I was afraid to enter, they stared at me so. Gaining courage, however, I crept inside. My little heart was panting for something I had not got. I wept while they sang the praises of God. I can never forget the words they sang—

"God is in heaven. Would He hear
A little prayer like mine?
Yes, dearest child, you need not fear,
He'd listen unto thine.

God is in heaven. Would He know
If I should tell a lie?
Yes, though you said it very low,
He'd hear it in the sky."

I then felt that I was a sinner, and that God knew everything about me. My heart seemed broken as I thought of my wickedness. I have discovered since that it was the Spirit of God working even in a poor little gipsy lad's heart. I found out that God is no respecter of persons, and that down in the human heart there are chords that once touched, will yield responsively. The governess came to me and asked what I was crying for. I told her I felt that I was a a very wicked boy; but instead of telling me of Jesus's love she gave me the cane.

The winter passed away, and my father being

better, we resumed our roaming gipsy life. On reaching Morden, in Cambridgeshire (it was on the Sunday), the Primitive Methodists were holding camp meetings close to our tents, and the Spirit of God drew me near to hear them. At night they held a prayer meeting in a cottage, and I found myself in their midst on my knees crying, when an old lady put her hand on my shoulder and said, "Jesus loves you, my boy," and talked to me very kindly about "His love." I did not find Him then—I could not understand. I had never been sent to school or taught to read, but the conviction was deep in my soul in those early days. "Bless the Lord O my soul," for His love to me a poor wandering gipsy boy. This is the fulfilment of John xvi., 8, 9 verses. When He shall come "He will reprove the world of sin, and of righteousness, and of judgment: of sin, because they believe not on me."

As I got older the passion for my fiddle and company grew, and I often frequented the dance room. The publican's flattery and "treats" made me think a great deal of myself. Of course I can see it now. I was bringing the publican gain, and helping to drag young and old further down into misery and sin. I was soon a great attraction, and sought for far and near, and in many places they would have no one else to play in their dancing and club rooms.

I remember one morning saying to my dear mother, "I am going to leave you, and shall go to London." She looked at me with astonishment. Putting her hands together, while tears rolled down her cheeks, she looked up to heaven and said, "My child will break my heart." I have never forgotten that look. It burnt its way into my soul, and left an impression there that lives to-day. In the public-house and skittle-alley, at card table, theatre, or boxing booth, the words, "You will break your mother's heart," were constantly ringing in my ears. I have often gone from these dens asking God to have mercy on a wretch like me, but sin had so tightly bound its chains around me that I had no power to break away. I was led captive by the devil at his will, and often knew with bitterness that "the way of transgressors is hard." I did not stay in London very long but made my way through the villages and towns to Cambridge, spending my time in riotous living—some nights sleeping in a bed and others on a straw stack. When I awoke from my bed on the hayrick I had to run up and down the road to promote circulation of the blood, my limbs being numbed with cold. I often said, like the prodigal, "I will arise and go to my father," for there was bread enough and to spare, while I was without shelter and perishing in the cold. But my poor soul had no refuge in the time of storm. How good God was to suffer me to live in utter rebellion against Him. He might have cut me down as a cumberer of the ground, but He willeth not the death of a sinner, but rather that he should repent and live.

I have been at the point of death several times—three times with fever; and once I was so very low that the power of speech deserted me for three weeks, and they had to put on me a strait jacket. The doctor said that if I lived until he got to his surgery and back it would be a miracle, but before he returned a change had taken place, and God had opened my mouth. I called "Mother." My mother cried out with much joy, "My boy has revived." From that hour I rapidly grew better. How good God is!

He has indeed dealt with me in mercy and not in wrath.

After that severe illness I had to go about on crutches for three weeks or a month; and as I gained strength from day to day, I formed resolutions in my mind to be better than I had been, but, alas, only to break them again and again—indeed, human nature in its best form is helpless until it brings its helplessness to God's almightiness. Should this book fall into the hands of any who are continually resolving and breaking their vows I would say, cast yourself in faith at His feet until He speaks the word of power.

After that long illness I stayed at home with my father and mother, and although it was only a gipsy's tent it was as much a home to me as your house is to you, or as a palace to a king. With all our wanderings we had this advantage—we took our home with us. My father taught me the same trade as himself, viz., mending cane chairs, and hawking. In the summer months we worked in the harvest field, my father having taught me to reap also. We worked for fifteen seasons for a Mr. Iviet, Hadenham, Cambridgeshire, and were known in that neighbourhood for upwards of twenty-five years. Since that time God has helped me and my two brothers to go there and preach Christ, and many have professed to find the gift of God, which is Christ Himself.

On one occasion we arrived at Newmarket during the fair time. After three days' frolic and drinking (by this time I had become a slave to drink and sin) my father fell in with a man who offered, if he desired company, to show him the way to Norwich. Agreeing to his proposal we started off, hawking our goods as we travelled through the villages and towns. On Saturday we arrived at a town called Swaffham, in Norfolk. It was market day, and as usual we commenced drinking, and I played the fiddle. The horses and carts stood outside the public-house. Towards evening my father said to me, "If we are to have any tents pitched to-night, and if we have any love for mother, we must go and do it at once." We at once left for one of the commons close by. My brother and the man that had been our guide stayed in the village drinking, coming home to us after the public-house was closed. On their way home they met a cart, and going behind it took out a basket of shop goods. My brother asked the man not to take it. He would have nothing to do with it, as my father was very strict about such things. The basket however was hidden somewhere close by. The first thing on Sunday morning one of the people who came to our tent said the policeman was coming, as the owner of the basket maintained that the gipsies had stolen it out of his cart. I asked my brother if he had taken it, and he said he had not, but went off with the thief, leaving us to get out of the charge the best way we could. I stayed with my father and mother, little thinking that they would take me, being perfectly innocent. In about an hour the policeman and the man who had lost his basket drew up to the tent in a trap, and declared that I was one who was "wanted." My parents protested against my arrest, knowing that I was innocent, but to no purpose. The handcuffs were put on, and I was compelled to go to the police station, along with a younger brother. We were brought before the magistrates and sent for trial to Swaffham, where we were detained a whole month before the trial took place. That was the first time I had been locked up. I was then between eighteen and nineteen years of age. Someone had told me that if I betrayed the man who had stolen the goods my brother would become involved in the crime; and rather than bring him in (for I loved my brother) I determined to bear the punishment instead. Being innocent, I felt I could bear it better than the guilty. At length my trial came on, and I received sentence, which was two months' hard labour, my younger brother being acquitted. The man who gave evidence against me declared on oath that I was the man who took the basket out of his cart. My dear father put his hands together in the court and declared my innocence, and said, "God will be your friend, my child." So you see, dear reader, that I suffered—the innocent for the guilty. So has Christ our Saviour suffered, the just for the unjust, that He might bring us to God. Oh what love, what boundless love! It is immeasurable! May you appreciate it, and love and serve Him in return.

I have heard men say that they could not leave off smoking and drinking; but a gaol is the place to wean them. They there make you non-smokers and abstainers from intoxicants by Act of Parliament, and without a pledge-book—at least I found it so. I had to leave it off whether I would or no.

The next morning they put me on the treadmill. I did not understand it, and soon fell down and hurt myself, while they stood round laughing at me. The weather was bitterly cold, and the prison clothing so thin that the wind seemed to pierce me through. Being afterwards put to work at an iron crank, I shammed bad and let go, which upset the machinery. The officers, with great consideration, took me before the doctor, who said I was not well, and gave me two pills, which I have cause to remember, and I was then sent to my cell. The prison rules required that at night our shoes and stockings should be placed at the head of the bed; but owing to the extreme cold I kept mine on to keep my feet warm. The warder on night duty coming round and missing both stockings and shoes, stripped the bed and drew me on to the flagstones, and left me in the dark to do the best I could. I shouted for a light to make my bed, but without any response.

In the morning I was again removed—this time to another cell, where there were five other prisoners. I there had to lie in a hammock, and I slept between the blankets instead of the sheets, experience having taught me which would be most comfortable. They tried to drag me out, but like a badger in a box, being in I had no inclination to come out—another thing they could not get me out. They reported me the next morning. I was then shut up in my cell, and my skilley was stopped. Oh, how I wept and reflected on my past life. I fell upon my knees, and promised God that if He spared me to come out of this horrible place I would lead a different life, and be careful as to the company I kept in the future.

Sunday morning came, and we were marched round the yard to the chapel, taking our different places in a little box arranged so that the prisoners could not see each other. My eyes were fixed on the chaplain. Taking up the Bible, he read the tenth chapter of St. John's Gospel. The fourteenth verse says, "I am the Good Shepherd, and know my sheep, and am known of mine." He made a running comment on this verse. He asked who was the Good Shepherd, and then said it was Jesus, that we were the sheep and that He laid down His life for us. I could not then understand it, but the Spirit of God was working in my heart. He then proceeded with the lesson, and commented on the sixteenth verse, "Other sheep I have, which are not of this fold: them also I must bring." The service being ended I went back to my cell, and my reflections ran thus: Christ has sheep in the fold, but I am one of those that are outside. But He meant to bring me in I felt sure. I was so deeply distressed, and cried to God to save me, that had there been anyone there to have pointed me to Christ, to rest on the promise of God, I most assuredly should have been converted. As it was I did not get peace. My term of imprisonment having passed away, both father and mother met me on being discharged. But alas! good resolutions formed in prison were soon again drowned in drink and bad company. Forgetting God in my wildest moments, I can truly say in the midst of it all the Holy Spirit continually strove with me. I became altogether reckless at this time, caring for nothing only the pleasures of this life, and spending my money as fast as I got it.

I remember, on one occasion, my sweetheart came to see me, and I was in such a state that I was ashamed to meet her. There was a field of cole and mustard seed close by, in which I lay down and hid myself, but by peering through the hedge I could see her and hear the conversation. Bad as I was I wanted to see her. My clothes, however, were so ragged that I feared to make an appearance. The following morning I went to Newmarket with seven shillings in my pocket—all the money I had. I entered a second-hand clothes shop and spent the money as best I could. When I saw my sweetheart she said I looked like a jockey. I began to be diligent from that day, as I thought of taking to myself a wife. This I did when we had got on a little, so that we were comfortably fixed.

One day, soon after our marriage, I went to Baldock, Hertfordshire, to a fair, and took a nice donkey with me to sell. Having sold it, I spent the money in drink. When I got home my wife asked me for the money, and I told her it had all been spent in drink. She scolded me, and I promised to do better, but I soon forgot my vows, and broke them, because they were made in my own strength. I had regular places where I played the fiddle for dancing and the amusement of the drunkards at the fairs and feasts, and was paid well, but the money came easily and it went freely. In those days I was called a jolly fellow—a nickname for a fool.

We travelled on to London, and keeping steady I soon got another donkey and cart to carry my tent and all the goods I had. Then we went into Kent for the hop-picking season, which was our harvest. There our first child was born. After the hopping season we made our way back to Cambridge, then to Newmarket fair, where revelling in drink was the order of the day. Here a row began. A young gipsy struck my father, and the devil worked me up to such a pitch that I would fight him. We fought until the blood ran like water. I have often thought of that battle. If one of us had been killed, what would the end have been? For me it would have been banishment from the presence of the Lord. In that battle I broke the small bone of my hand, the effect of which is felt and seen to this day. Again I knew that "the way of transgressors is hard." Years afterwards, when God had converted me, I went to this man and told him that God had saved me, and how I loved him and wanted him to be saved too. He wept like a child, and cried for mercy, and then and there with his wife trusted Christ as his Saviour. They had lived together many years unmarried, and as soon as the Lord opened their eyes they set their home in order, and were married, living godlylives. He, poor fellow, went to heaven through much affliction. In his dying moments he took my hand and pointed upward. Although he could not speak he made us know it was all right. Like myself he was a brand plucked from the burning. Oh, the joy of bringing ost souls to Christ.

We were now at Melbourne, in Cambridgeshire. I was out one morning early after my horses. Coming home I picked up a few sticks and some straw to make a fire. The policeman saw me, and he said I had stolen them, and I was his prisoner. He took hold of me by the handkerchief round my neck. I then thought it was my turn, and I threw him on his back into the ditch. He got up and went away, saying he would have me dead or alive. He fetched some help, and I was taken to Cambridge, and placed in a cell next to a man who was condemned to be hung, for burning a woman to death. He had pleaded "not guilty," which caused the authorities much anxiety. The governor put me to walk with him in the yard, as they wanted me to hear what he had to say about the crime. I found out by his conversation he was guilty, for he told me he was with the woman, and four of them drank a little bucket of gin. Here again you see the evil of strong drink—"it biteth like a serpent, and stingeth like an adder." Young men, shun it! One day his poor wife came in to see him for the last time. She had a little baby in her arms. Holding it up to him she said, "Look at your baby," and then asked, "What is to become of me, John, and my three children?" He put up his hands and said, "Have mercy upon me, for my wife and children's sake! I never thought it would come to this." How true it is, "The wages of sin is death." I wept at that scene, and being taken back to my cell, I cried to God to have mercy on a guilty sinner like me. My relief was great after I had my trial, and was told that I was to have a month with hard labour. My prison occupation was that of winding string into balls, for the purpose of mat making. As it was extremely cold, I formed them into an armchair, in which I sat, to keep myself warm. Reflection again seized me, for there is plenty of time to think there. My sins again seemed as if they would crush me, and I was again on my knees before God, crying for deliverance, and obtained some relief. Just then the keeper came in, and told me to hold my noise. Being ignorant of the plan of salvation, and having no one to instruct me, the good impressions soon passed away, and I returned to my old habits of sin and waywardness. How good of God it was to spare me, and not to cut me off as a cumberer of the ground! But He had compassion, that He might show forth His glory in me, and at length enable me to witness a good profession before many witnesses. Bless Him for ever! He is my refuge and strength.

CHAPTER II.

SHADOWS GATHERING—SMALLPOX AND DEATH.

SEVERAL years passed away, but I still continued the same wandering life. By this time I was the father of five children. Resting near Town-Malden, in Essex, I had risen early one morning to look after my horses. I found one in the ditch with its back broken, and had to sell him for dogs meat. This was a great trouble to me at the time. The reader must learn that even a gipsy has his peculiar troubles; we are born to them as the sparks fly upwards. We travelled on to Epping Forest, where we found a gipsy by the name of Cooper, whose wife's mother lay dead, and he asked me if I would keep their company, as they were all alone. I consented, but the husband of the dead woman ran away, leaving the corpse with us. He left no money behind him with which to bury his wife, although he had made arrangements with the undertaker for the coffin and burial. Of course that individual wanted paying. There was nothing left, however, but the goods and chattels of the runaway, and they had to be taken or nothing, and he held possession until the bill was paid. These little incidents are given to show how cruel and unsympathetic some men are, and all this had a tendency to show me the unreality of the world. The man subsequently came back and paid the bill. Very probably he could not rest, knowing that his dead wife was not buried. His goods were then restored to him, but he charged us with cheating him. In the morning, when I went to look for my horse it wa gone; and then I looked for the man, but, to my astonishment, he was likewise missing. I at once came to the conclusion that he had taken my horse and decamped, and immediately went in search, advertised for the horse, and walked about seeking it for about a week, until I was fairly broken down in health. About a fortnight after a policeman came to me, and said a horse answering to the description I gave was then in Westminster Green Yard. I went to see it, and recognised it as mine, but it was little to my advantage, for it had to be sold to pay expenses; and when sold, to my chagrin my share only amounted to two shillings and sixpence. Having lost my horse, I had nothing to draw my gipsy van with. There was nothing therefore left for me but to sell out and again take to a tent. I bought a pony and cart, which cost me five pounds; a set of harness for fifteen pence, which you may be sure needed some repairing. Having got some wax ends, I set to work to make the best of it. During repairs I again thought of my folly, and longed for a change and brighter days. Having once more succeeded in making another start in this roaming life, we were again on the road. Fortune again seemed to smile, and I was enabled to purchase a living-van. But trouble had not left us yet, for although gipsies, and not accustomed to remain in one place long together, yet trouble followed us and found us out. Although at that time I could not understand why I was beset on every hand with darkness, now that the clouds have dispersed, and the Sun of Righteousness has risen, I can see it was God's providential hand that was leading me by a way that I knew not.

We had travelled to Baldock, Herts, and we stayed in a wide lane called the highway, when my eldest child fell ill with smallpox. The doctor ordered us to go into one of the by-lanes away from the town, where I built up a tent for my dear wife and children, and took the van about two hundred yards from them and used it as an hospital. Had we not been gipsies very probably they would have taken the girl to the local hospital. But, alas for us! we were gipsy outcasts. I had to act as the attendant for the sick one, and so I watched and nursed. This was in the month of March, as far as I can recollect. At that time I could neither read nor write, so that I have very little recollection as to dates. My wife used to bring the food halfway between the van and the tent; and sometimes before I could get there it would be covered with snow. Oh, how she used to weep and say, "My poor child will die," and "I shall never get over this." Soon afterwards my son was seized with the disease. Trouble upon trouble came upon our gipsy home, and so I brought the van near to the tent, and for one whole month I never had my clothes off. One after the other fell sick with the smallpox, and I had to do the best I could for the whole of them. It may be that you, dear reader, know something of trial, and of nursing the sick and watching the dying ones as they breathe their last. God only knows what I went through during that time of trial. My dear wife was stricken, and then a baby was born. Was not this trouble? I saw that she was dying, and as I sat by her side I asked her if she was afraid to die, and if she thought of God. She said "Yes; but when I am praying to God, a great black hand comes before me, and shows me all the wicked things I have done, and something says, 'There is no mercy for you.'" But I had great assurance that God would forgive her. So I spoke to her again, and told her about Christ, and asked her to look to Him; that He was her Saviour, and that He died for sinners. On Sunday she seemed to be much calmer, and looking into my face, said with a smile, "I want you to promise me one thing. Will you be a good father to my children?" I promised her that I would. She put her arms round my neck and kissed me, and rested peacefully in the bed. In the evening, rallying herself, she sang—

"I have a Father in the promised land.
My God calls me, I must go,
To meet Him in the promised land."

I watched her through the night, for she was sinking very fast. On Monday morning she seemed to be all the while praying. About eight o'clock she breathed her last, and although a gipsy, I believe she is gone to heaven, for where there is nothing given, nothing will be required. But I was left with six motherless children, the baby being only five days old. My children hearing that their mother was dead, ran out of the tent crying, "What shall we do? We have no mother now!" My heart was pierced—something within told me that she was gone to heaven, and I was on my way to hell. I had some light and knowledge to point her to Christ, but had no Christ myself.

On Tuesday night, between ten and eleven o'clock, I followed her to the grave, by a lantern light, the only mourner. She was buried in a place called Norton, near Baldock. I do not know how I got back. My trouble was more than I could bear, and my sorrow was great. At midnight, I went into a plantation beside my van, and threw myself on my face. When all was still, I asked God to help me to keep the promise I had made to my dying wife. God did help me, as far as this life goes; and my sister's daughter came to me to nurse the baby.

During the afternoon of the day I buried my wife my niece was doing some washing, and the tent got on fire, and burnt it quite down, which left the children without anything to put on. The sparks were flying all over the coffin, the children crying, "Oh, my mother will be burnt up." My strength seemed to fail me. I fell on my face in the grass, weeping like a child, not knowing what to do. I rushed into the fire to try and save what I could, but the flames were so great that I was forced to escape and let it burn itself out. The van was saved. God most wonderfully upheld me under this great trial, and I did not take the disease. A fortnight after the poor little baby died, and was buried beside its mother. We remained in that lane a few weeks longer; then the doctor gave me leave to move on, all danger being over. So we took farewell of the place where we had seen so much sorrow, and I made up my mind to be a different man, but trying in my own strength failed again and again.

CHAPTER III.

CONVERSION OF MYSELF, TWO BROTHERS, AND MANY OTHER GIPSIES.

I ALWAYS said my prayers night and morning, and asked God to give me power over drink, and sin, and self, but failed as often as the temptation came to me. I was like the chaff driven before the wind. I often groaned before the Lord, and hated myself after every defeat, because so easily overcome; and not being able to read the Word of God, never having been to school, it was no wonder that I was ignorant of the way of life.

About this time I became so concerned about my soul that I seemed to rest nowhere. I travelled through Bedfordshire and around to London, to see my father and mother, and they helped me in my trouble with my children for a little time. Then my sister and her husband accompanied us with their van, and as they had no children of their own, she was like a mother to mine, and he was kind as a father to them. My sister could read the New Testament, and used to read to me about the sufferings of Christ, and His death upon the tree for sinful man. She told me it was the sins of the people that nailed Him there, and I often felt in my heart that I was one of them. She was deeply moved when I wept, and said, "Oh how cruel to serve Him so." I took farewell of them, but left my youngest child with them for a time, and travelled on to High Barnett, and made tracks for Luton, Bedfordshire. All the while I was very lonely and sad at heart, and often when my children were asleep, and my horses put away for the night, I have wrestled and struggled on the ground before God with the powers of darkness, but found no relief. It was like the troubled sea casting up mire and dirt. If ever there was a soul that understood the meaning of wormwood and gall, I did.

One morning, just before we reached Luton, I had left a daughter to hawk her goods, and told her I would wait for her on the roadside with my van. While waiting, I looked up and saw two vans approaching from Luton. To my great delight it was my two brothers, Woodlock and Bartholomew; who were equally delighted and surprised to meet me. We began to talk, and I found that they were in the self-same trouble about their souls. God was dealing with them and convincing them of sin. How wonderful are the dealings of God with the children of men. As we talked, we felt how nice it would be to settle down, and go to God's house and learn of Him—for I had got tired of my roaming life. The more we talked about it the stronger the conviction grew, and we resolved to be different men, whatever the consequences might be. My brothers turned round and went with me to Cambridge. Upon arrival, we went to a public-house, and told the landlady how we felt. She began to weep, and said, "I have a book upstairs that will just suit you, for it makes me cry every time I read it." She went upstairs, and brought it down, and lent it to us to read. We went out into the road to mind our horses, and a young man came out to read the book to us. As he read, our convictions grew stronger. We felt, like its author (it was "Bunyan's Pilgrim's Progress"), that we wanted to get rid of our burden. My brother Bartholomew rose up and said, "If God does not save me I shall die." All of us felt the smart of sin at that moment and wept like little children. We returned the book, and thanked the woman for lending it to us. Sad to relate, soon after this, her husband, coming home the worse for drink, was thrown out of his trap and killed on the spot. I felt it was another warning for me, and praised God, in my way, that I had been spared.

On Sunday we went to the Primitive Methodist Chapel, Fitzroy Street, Cambridge, morning, afternoon, and night. At night Mr. Guns preached. His points were very cutting to my soul; he seemed to aim directly at me. I tried to hide myself behind a pillar in the chapel, but he, looking and pointing in that direction, said, "He died for thee." The anxious ones were asked to come forward; and in the prayer meeting the preacher came to where I was sitting, and asked me if I was saved. I cried out, "No! that is what I want." He tried to show me that Christ had paid my debt; but the enemy of souls had blinded my eyes, and made me believe that I must first feel it and then believe it, instead of receiving Christ by faith first. Thousands make a great mistake there. I went from that house of prayer still a convicted sinner, but not a converted one.

I again travelled to London, to Epping Forest, to see my father and mother, who were there encamping in their tent. I put my horses in a piece of enclosed ground, and on Monday, when I went to fetch them out, the Spirit of God told me it was wrong. I told God that that should be the last time I would ever do such a thing, or sin against Him knowingly. I then told my father and mother, brothers and sisters, and some of the gipsy tribe, that I was done with roaming and wrong-doing, and that I meant to turn to God, by His help. How they looked at me and wept. My eldest brother, who was weeping, said, "My brother is going to heaven and I am going to hell." My two brothers, Woodlock and Bartholomew, sold their horses to a man, but the man lent them the horses after he had bought them, that they might take their vans through London to Shepherd's Bush, on a piece of building land close to Mr. Henry Varley's chapel. Brother

Woodlock went to take the horses back to the man who lent them, and while he was away I sold mine, being determined to have no hindrance, as I meant to settle down and find Christ, if He was to be found. Bless Him! He saw that I was in earnest; and the Spirit of God told me I should be saved that night. And so I was, with my dear brother Bartholomew. After I got my van settled I built up my tent, and then I asked God to direct me to some place where I might learn the way to heaven. I could think of nothing else but Christ. I believed His blood was shed for me—yes, for me, a poor gipsy—and not only for me, but for you, dear reader; yes, for all the world. Praise His name.

I inquired of a young man if he could direct me to a place where there was going to be a service that night. He said, "Yes." Just then a young man stepped up and said, "Are you going to be religious?" I said, "I don't know anything about being religious; what I want is Christ, and Christ I will have before I come back." This man was so angry at my determination being so great that he said he would be a very devil in the midst of us. I went off to the meeting, my brother Bartholomew going with me. We found a little mission hall in Latimer Road, Shepherd's Bush. It was a prayer meeting, and several working men were there. They were singing that good old hymn—

"There is a fountain filled with blood."

As they were singing the power of God took hold of me. I was standing up, and my mind seemed to be taken away from everybody and fixed heavenward. It seemed as if I was bound in a chain and they were drawing me up to the ceiling. I was unconscious until I fell on the floor, and they told me afterwards that I lay there wallowing and foaming for half an hour, like the son that the father brought to Jesus (Mark ix. 17). When I came to myself, I seemed to hear the voice of Jesus saying, "Thou dumb and deaf spirit, come out of him and enter him no more," and the spirit rent me sore, and came out that same hour. Some of my children were there, and, crying, said, "Oh, dear, our father is dead!" Blessed be His name, I had only then commenced to live! My bands fell off, my tongue was loosed, and I immediately rose and told the people that Christ had saved me. My dear brother Bartholomew was saved the same night. No human instrument pointed me the way; God began it and God finished it. I told the people that my wife had been dead three years, and that I had been under deep conviction ever since that time. The change was so great that I walked about the hall, looking at my flesh. To me it did not seem the same colour. My burden was gone, and I told the people that I felt so light that if the room had been full of eggs I could have walked through and not have broken one of them. Glory be to God for His wondrous way in dealing with me. I went forth a new creature in Him. When I arrived home my children were called, and, for the first time in that gipsy home, I knelt with them in prayer. I began at the right place—with my dear children. I shall never forget that night how I sang; and well I might, when such a sinner as I had been was delivered from my guilt. My joy was indeed great, and I told my children that "old things had passed away," and that we must lead a new life together. I did not sleep much that night. I was talking to Jesus, and asking Him how I should go on. A voice seemed to say, "Now are ye clean." I said, "It is enough,

Lord. My soul believes it. What must I do to keep clean?" A voice came again, "Abide in me." I did not know at that time that it was in the Bible, but you will find it in John xv. 3, 4. Oh, how sweet it sounded to my soul! I was lost in wonder, love, and praise, and fell asleep singing,

"My Jesus, I love Thee,
I know Thou art mine."

In the morning I went on my knees in my gipsy van and asked God to guide me by His Spirit to live as He would have me, for I was willing to obey Him. Going outside and looking round the van, I thought I never saw anything look so new and bright. My brother Woodlock came to me and asked me how I had been saved, for he had heard the news. I told him I was a new man, that I had found a peace as calm as a river, and that Jesus had cast out the evil spirit. He replied, "Yours is a real conversion." The devil made my statement a snare for him, telling him that he must feel just exactly as I felt or he would not be converted, so he was kept in bondage till the following Sunday. After breakfast I again prayed with my children, and asked God to save them, receiving an impression while I was praying that I must go and speak to the other gipsies that were encamped on the same piece of ground, numbering about twenty families. Being quite willing to take up my cross I obeyed and went, when in their midst I began to sing, and I told them what great things the Lord had done for me. Many of them were bathed in tears. I turned round to my brother Bartholomew's van, and saw him and his wife on their knees, and she was crying to God for mercy. God saved her there and then. My brother Bartholomew and I then commenced a prayer meeting in one of the gipsy tents, and my eldest son and daughter were brought to Christ that morning, with several others, until thirteen gipsies professed to find Christ as their Saviour. I shall never forget our first prayer meeting. We were like the woman at the well, crying, "Come, see a man that told me all things that ever I did. Is not this the Christ?" The prayer meeting ended, and there was a calm.

Now commenced a new life. My attention was first drawn to my fiddle, that I had played and loved in the dancing saloons; and so that it should form no temptation to me, I made up my mind to part with it, although it had brought me in great gain. I took it to a pawnshop in Shepherd's Bush, and asked the broker what he would give for it, as I wished to sell it. He said, "What! sell your best friend?" I told him I had found Jesus, and He had taken away all desire for worldly things. He wept, and taking my hand said, "May God bless you," and we parted. This was April the 6th, 1869.

Mr. Henry Varley, of Notting Hill, heard of our conversion and came to invite us to his tabernacle. We accepted his invitation and received considerable help from his preaching. He put a mission tent on the ground where we were staying, and called it the "Gipsy Tabernacle." A lady volunteered to teach the gipsy children in the daytime, and several young men came in the evening to give us an hour's reading, and to hold services on different nights in the week. On April 11th, 1869, my dear brother Woodlock found Christ in Mr. Varley's vestry, and joined us in praising God. At this time the devil began to rage. Seeing he had lost three of his servants he did his best to upset us, and we were all turned off the ground where we had been staying. Some of the friends told me to hire a field. I did so, at a rent of £25 per annum. We moved our tents and vans into this field, and all the gipsies went with us. The tents were pitched all round the field, with the mission tent in the centre. Meetings were continually held, and we had every opportunity to testify to our gipsy riends what the Lord had done for us. But the enemy had not done with us. Several of the gipsies' antagonists got drunk, fought, and made a great disturbance; and as we had paid no deposit on the land we were again expelled.

We went to God in prayer, and asked His guidance in the matter, as we three brothers were determined to work for God. I was led to a farmhouse close by. Knocking at the door, the gentleman came out and asked me what I wanted. I told him the Lord had sent me to ask him to let us come under the railway arch that was in the corner of his field. He said he was afraid to let us come in. I assured him that we were honest, and that he might use our horses—for we had bought more to enable us to go to Kent for the hop season, where we had worked for Mr. Hodge, Orphan Green, for many years. He seemed at a standstill, not knowing what to do. His wife then came out and entreated him on our behalf, and he yielded and gave me the key. We stayed there until September. He found work for us, and we had some precious times all the while we were there. We still kept going to Mr. Varley's tabernacle until we left for Kent, proving that "godliness is profitable for all things, having the promise of this life and that which is to come." Soon after we wrote to my father and mother, telling them we were converted, and then went to see them at Lowton Forest. They soon prepared something for us to eat. We told them that before we partook of food now we prayed. All knelt down, and my father cried for mercy, and said he ought to have set the example. Instead of that, we had come to teach him; and both father and mother rested upon the promise of God. They were then seventy years of age. They lived five years after that, trusting in the finished work of Christ.

I have already intimated that we went down to Kent during the hopping season. This time someone had already told my master that his fancy men had turned religious. He replied that he was very glad to hear it. When I met him at the farm he said, "Good morning. I have heard good news." I told him at once that I had found Christ. He gripped my hand, and the tears stood in his eyes. He said, "You must come up to the house to-night, and then we can talk more about it." We accordingly went, sang some hymns, and talked about our conversion, and the power of God fell upon us. His wife said we had better turn it into a prayer meeting. We were soon on our knees, and I believe from that time several of that family were savingly converted to God. They built us a tent in the cherry orchard, and we held services right through the hopping season. The work was so blessed that Mr. Varley came down to help us. The policeman who was told off on duty there was told to take his staff with him. He replied to his superintendent that he would much rather take his Bible, for the gipsy was preaching Jesus, and such had been the change produced that the staff was not required. More blessed to relate, the policeman and his daughter were converted during the services there. Praise God!

At Michaelmas, the season being over, we made tracks once more for Cambridge, to settle down for the winter on a piece of ground near the Gas House in Barnwell. On Sunday we commenced to sing the praises of God outside near our vans, and very soon a crowd of people congregated round us. We talked to them of Jesus and His love, and invited them to the chapel. We went off singing, the people following us, and the chapel was soon full. We never lost the influence of that meeting. All glory to our risen Saviour, who hath chosen the weak things of this world to confound the mighty.

CHAPTER IV.

WORK AMONG THE CHURCHES.

It soon got spread abroad that the converted gipsies were preaching Christ. I told them God had brought us out of darkness into His wonderful light, and we now wanted to work for Him. The Primitives took us by the hand first and put us on their plan, and we laboured for God all over the circuit, in the Wesleyan and Baptist mission rooms, in the ragged schools, and in the mission room with Mr. Sykes. Upwards of a hundred souls professed to find Christ that winter. At Harston a publican found Christ, and came out of his public-house. The cottage services which we held on Wednesday seemed to stir me up so that I told God that if He would give me conversions I would always witness for Him whenever the opportunity presented itself. How I prayed about that first meeting that God would bless it! I had to walk twelve or fourteen miles, and as I went along I distributed tracts, and had a good chance to speak to many about their souls' welfare. Having reached a bylane, I stood still and began to preach to a field of turnips—getting ready for the meeting. It was a poor congregation; I could get no response; they had neither eyes nor ears; but to my astonishment there were two men the other side of the hedge that I had not seen, who had overheard my discourse. Thank God it did not prove in vain, for they came for ward and thanked me for what they had heard. I went to the meeting with my heart full of joy and the little place was packed. A young man who would not go anywhere to hear the way of life came to hear the gipsy. God's Spirit took hold of him and he was converted that night, and afterwards became a local preacher. So God sealed my labours and gave me that one soul, and he is still working for Jesus with all his heart.

Having finished our meetings in Cambridge, the friends presented us with the first Bibles that we ever had in our lives. Our final meetings were held in the very ragged school where God had convinced me of sin when but a child. Some of my children had occasionally gone to school since my conversion, and had therefore learned to read the Bible to me. Being uneducated and thirsting for the Word of Life this was marrow and fatness to my soul, a lamp unto my feet, and a light to my path. My desire to read the Bible was at this time very great, so I went alone into my van, knelt down before the Lord, and said, "O Lord, Thou hast made me, and Thou canst teach me to read Thy Word," and God did help me, and I soon learned to spell out for myself, and so claim the promises as my own.

From Cambridge we made our way to London, calling at the Forest, as was our custom every year, and then on to Canning Town, to the place called Chevvy Island. There was always a number of gipsies encamped on this ground. On Sunday a singing band of men and women from a camp meeting came into our encampment. They were all arranged on a large wagon. We were delighted at having the people of God with us. True we were strangers to them at first, but afterwards found out that they were the Christian Mission, and were soon at home amongst them. It soon reached the ears of Mr. W. Booth that there were three converted gipsy brothers in their camp. He did not take long before he sought an interview with us; and, taking us by the hand, gave us encouragement, and said the way to keep bright and happy was to work for God. We took his advice and cast our lot in with them, and were put upon their plan as the "Three Converted Gipsies," and were owned of God wherever we went, even to the salvation of numbers of precious souls. The outcome of the effort put forth during our short stay with the mission will only be known in eternity.

About the month of November we returned again to Cambridge, and our hearts were gladdened when we saw many still holding on their way that had been brought to Christ the previous winter. Again we commenced work for God, and gipsies, college gentlemen, and others, were seen marching through the streets singing,

"There is a fountain filled with blood," &c.,

the outcome of which was a genuine revival. The

The work was so great that we had to give up working at our trades, and invitations became so pressing that we felt the call was from God, so we left our chair-caning and basket-mending and gave ourselves wholly and solely to the work of saving souls.

Our first invitation was to Biggleswade, in Bedfordshire. Mr. Sounday found us a meadow in which to put our vans. The engagement was for a week, but the work of God broke out so vigorously that we had to stay a month, and one hundred souls professed to have given themselves to Christ.

From there we went to Potton and Gamblinggay, and everywhere signs and wonders were wrought in the name of the Holy Child Jesus. Many are to be found to-day in that neighbourhood who remember the visit of the converted gipsies to the praise of God. In the midst of our work we received a letter from the Rev. Wm. Booth, wishing us to go right into the work of the Lord under the auspices of the Christian Mission. It was a matter of consideration for me, for I keenly felt my unfitness for this work; but God's strength was made perfect in weakness. My dear brothers were one in mind with me, and after waiting upon the Lord for guidance we again started for London. On our way Mr. Booth met us at Baldock, Hertfordshire, and we talked the matter over and prayed together, and he said that after much prayer he wanted us to go to Portsmouth, and I should have to have a fiddle again and use it for God. I felt willing to do anything and go anywhere if it would glorify God and bring souls to Christ. We met Mr. Booth in London at the end of three weeks, at the People's Hall, Whitechapel, and he told us that the bills were out in Portsmouth announcing that the three converted gipsies with their hallelujah fiddle were coming.

At Portsmouth the services were held in a large theatre, and God again owned our labours. We afterwards went to Gosport, just at the time when the soldiers were returning from the Ashantee War. Many meetings were held there and God blessed the Word, and many of the soldiers were brought to know the Lord as their Saviour. One of the soldiers said in his experience, that whilst fighting out there in the bush, his comrades falling down on either side of him, he was struck in the chest with a slug from the enemy, and had it not been for his mother's Bible which he carried in his breast-pocket, he would assuredly have been numbered with the slain. "My life was saved," he said; "but, blessed be God, now He has saved my soul." We had some remarkable meetings there, and on leaving Mr. Cook presented us each with a Bible as a grateful memento of our visit.

Proceeding to Southampton with Brother Corbridge, crowded meetings were held in a large wooden circus, which would accommodate three thousand persons. At first the work was hard, and no results were seen, but we felt the Spirit of God was working. Thirteen came forward during the week, but we were so heavily burdened because so comparatively few yielded, that we went home and wept before the Lord because of their impenitence. But Mr. Corbridge cheered us and said, "We shall have them. They are feeling the smart of sin, and they are in pickle." Thank God He came to our relief, and one hundred souls came out for Christ. And so we were kept as the specials for the Christian Mission, being sent here and there. Having been sent to Chatham, one night it looked like a mighty battle. There were soldiers and sailors, black men and white men, rich men and poor men, all on their knees, crying before God, who is "no respecter of persons." He that feareth God, and worketh righteousness, whatever his nationality or colour, is accepted by Him. (Acts x.) One man was a greengrocer. The devil told him he would lose his customers if he shut his shop on Sunday. We told him that the Lord would make it up to him in other ways. He obtained a board, and had painted on it the words, "This shop will be closed on Sundays." I nailed it up tight for him, and we shouted, "Hallelujah! Christ has got the victory!"

About this time the invitations were so pressing that we were led to launch out independently, depending upon God entirely. Having related our conviction to Mr. Booth he saw the reasonableness of our case, and kneeling down commended us to the keeping of our Master. I then said, "Here is the fiddle that you gave me to play. You purchased it, and you have a right to it." He replied, "I shall not take it from you. Seeing that you are married to it, I make you a present of it to use in the Lord's work." We then bade each other good-bye, and from that day until now God has opened the door of usefulness to us, and we have depended upon Him, walking by faith and not by sight. "The harvest truly is great, but the labourers are few."

On one occasion the Lord impressed me very much about going to Bedford, although we had received no invitation. I told my two brothers how I felt about going. They said, "It is of the Lord, we will go at once." So we put our horses in our vans, and away we went for the town of Bedford. We had to take a place where we could stand our vans, after we had arrived in the town. We were charged nine shillings a week for the stand and nine shillings more for a field to put the horses in, making eighteen shillings, and we were not sure of a penny piece coming in; but believing as we did, that we were sent by God, we knew it would be all right. We went to see John Bunyan's statue; and as we gazed at it we asked God to use us in that town, even as He had used his servant John Bunyan in years gone by. From there we went to Bunyan's Chapel; and as we stood looking, the chapel-keeper asked us if we would like to see inside. We accepted his offer, and sat down in the very chair which this man of God had sat in, and asked God to give us power to do something for Him in Bedford. A brother in Christ who was standing there said, "You appear to be strangers to this part." We told him we were, but that we were not strangers to the Lord Jesus. I told him we were known as the three converted gipsies. He shed tears of joy, and said the Primitive Methodist minister wanted to see us, but he did not know in what part of the country we were in. We went to his house, and after talking the matter over he asked us if we would commence a week's special mission at once. We told him that was why we had arrived; and we began in the open air and sang to the chapel, which was soon crowded to the door, and the power of God fell upon us, and very many souls were brought to the Lord. Every night throughout the week God richly manifested His power in our midst, to the joy and salvation of very many precious souls. Oh, how mysterious is the hand of God! He led us and guided our steps, and blessed us there; and from that visit to Bedford sprang up invitation after invitation to visit the scenes of former labours. We afterwards went there for Mr. Usher, at the bank, and conducted services in the Bedford Hall, and God owned His Word and blessed our testimony to the salvation of not a few.

After our first visit to Bedford we left for Cambridge, to stay there for the winter, taking that as our centre. We received calls on every hand. We had an invitation to Baldock, Herts. Having put our horses in our vans we were soon on the road, making tracks for our destination. The roads were very bad and heavy. Night overtaking us we made a halt, and our horses were permitted to graze by the roadside. Before conversion we were not so particular. We found accommodation for them in someone else's field. But now we were made new creatures in Christ Jesus, and old things had passed away. About four o'clock in the morning I was surprised at some one knocking at my front door, and saying, "Hallo, there!" I replied from within, "Who are you?" He said, "I am the policeman, and have come to take you into custody." I said, "Why?" He replied, "There is a law made that if any gipsies are found stopping by the roadside for twelve miles round they are to be taken up without a summons or a warrant." I told him he must be careful in this case, as we were exceptions to the rule, being a King's children, and that the Bible said if they touched one of God's little ones they touched the apple of His eye. He said, "I'll wait until you get up." When I had dressed myself and gone out, I found there were four policemen awaiting us. We were handcuffed like felons and taken to the lockup. I told them there was no necessity to put the bracelets on us, as we should not run away; but they would not heed. The journey was rather lengthy, being one mile and a half to the lockups. All the way we preached to the policemen and told them that God would bring them to judgment if they neglected the Lord Jesus Christ, and that we should be witnesses against them at the great day, and would then declare that in the *name* of Jesus we had faithfully warned them to flee from the wrath to come. They never responded once, but trudged on in peculiar silence. They undoubtedly had not had such prisoners in their possession before, nor such a lengthy discourse, for that night I had preached to them a sermon "a mile and a half long." Arriving at the lockup, we were placed in the cell. We were soon on our knees in prayer, pleading with God to touch their hearts and save them as he did the gaoler of old. The Lord heard us, and the policemen wept. Then we began to sing—

"He breaks the power of cancelled sin,
He sets the prisoner free."

The keeper said we must not make such a noise. We asked him if ever he had read of Paul and Silas having been put into prison, and he said "Yes." Then I asked, "What did they do?" He answered, "They sang praises to God;" and I replied, "And so will we," and we struck up singing again—

"His blood can make the foulest clean,
His blood avails for me."

They found they had a queer lot of prisoners there at that early hour. The keeper gave us some rugs to keep us warm; and his wife came down weeping and said, "Who have you got here? I have been very much troubled ever since they came." The husband told her to make us some coffee hot, and to give us some bread and butter. Having done so, she brought it to us and I began to talk to her about her soul and about Jesus, and I gave her a little tract entitled "The blood of Jesus Christ cleanses from all sin." I told her the story of His death for sinners. She drank in every word, and there and then trusted Christ as her Saviour, and we again praised God together.

We were brought before the magistrates in the morning. We had no money on us; but we were fined twenty-five shillings each, or in default im prisonment for fourteen days. Our fines, however, were paid, and we went on our way to Baldock. We can see here that the devil wanted to hinder us in our work and mission at Baldock, but God richly blessed our visit to that place, and many were brought in who have since been working for Jesus. We told the people that we had all been locked up at Melbourne, and the news spread on every hand; but we afterwards received an invitation there, which we accepted. Our meetings were held in a meadow, and our friend the policeman was there, and several others. They were sent to keep order, as the crowds were very great, the attraction being the gipsies that had been locked up in that very town.

"God moves in a mysterious way,
His wonders to perform."

The amount of good that came out of this singular occurrence will only be known in eternity, for the Holy Spirit of God was mightily manifest.

I have previously said that Cambridge was to be our centre. On one occasion I was very busy working in the van. It was Christmas Eve. Being much impressed by the Spirit of God to work for Him, I went on my knees in prayer. I was thanking God for His goodness to me in all my former career, and so greatly did He bless me that I began to sing—

"In some way or other the Lord will provide."

Just then there was a knock at the van door. It was Mr. Sykes, the missionary, who came in, and shaking me by the hand said, "How good God is, isn't He?" "He is good," I replied. "Yes," he said. "I have come to tell you that there are three legs of mutton for you and your two brothers." I could not answer him for a moment, being taken by surprise. He told me the Lord had sent them, but we would have to fetch them from the grocer's shop at six o'clock. We were there in time, and as we entered the door I saw three bags of flour standing there also. I said to my brothers, "They are ours, I feel sure." They smiled and said, "Hold your tongue," but it turned out so to be. We were well supplied with provisions for the Christmas, and we never knew who payed for them from that day to this. But the Word of God is verified that "no good thing will He withhold from them that walk uprightly."

It will be interesting to the reader to follow me closely at this point of my story of a few details as to our missionary effort in several parts of the country, and the wonderful way that God opened the doors of usefulness for us, without any advertisement on our part. On one occasion a gentleman from Norwich came to Cambridge for a missionary meeting (Mr. Scott). Where he dined there were some who had recently given their hearts to Christ, and during the conversation over the table they told how they had been brought in through the instrumentality of the converted gipsies; and also as to the interest that still pervaded the town because of the meetings that were still being held. He desired an interview with the gipsies, and eventually they brought him to our vans, and the outcome of the interview was an invitation to Norwich.

Arriving on this battle-ground we commenced operations in the Dutch Church adjoining St. Andrew's Hall. We were there for eight days. The crowds were very great, and the Mayor of Norwich said we should have taken the St. Andrew's Hall to accommodate the people. Thank God, many were brought into personal contact with Christ through that mission. We returned in the year 1886, nearly eleven years after the first visit, and found many who held sweet remembrances of that time, who were still rejoicing in the hope that is set before them in the Gospel. We have repeatedly visited Norwich since, and we have no greater joy than to know that our children walk in the truth.

I remember too, with grateful remembrance, a visit that we paid to Wymondham, in Norfolk, during the ministry of Mr. Meddows (Primitive Methodist). The whole town seemed in one fervour of religious feeling. So mightily was the Holy Spirit's power manifested that we had not much time to eat our food. Great was the cry of convicted souls, and we believe the dear Lord healed them all. More than one hundred precious souls were brought to the Lord during that mission. Here the chapel was again too small, and we had to seek enlargement. Many of the young men who sought the Lord at that time are now preachers of the Gospel—so I have learnt from Mr. Lane, a good man of God. To the glory of His name, He can keep as well as save.

We also visited Hadingham, Cambridgeshire, labouring with Mr. James Smith, the Baptist minister. God owned our labours during that week to the salvation of many.

About this time we received an invitation to Leeds, to the York Street Chapel. Here some notable characters were savingly converted, one in particular, a soldier in Her Majesty's army. In relating his experience, he said that during a recent campaign he had been in attendance on two large guns, when the men all around him were falling in death. At that time he had never had a thought as to what would become of his soul if numbered with the slain.

God was far from his thoughts then, but now he was happy and a new creature in Christ. He was then living in a street which was known as "Little Hell." He said, "If I had died in my sin there is no doubt but that I should have been in a big hell." His wife also said, "God has indeed given me a new husband. My home since his change is like a little heaven below." A brother was also weeping at that meeting, and I asked him why he wept. He replied, "For joy," for all his class had been brought to Christ. We have been to Leeds four years in succession.

It is needless to take the reader any further in my travels up and down the land—suffice it to say that God has blessed the testimony, simple as it may have been, from the lips of three gipsies. God has backed His word with power, and letters on every hand have reached us expressive of gratitude to God that ever we came that way.

CHAPTER V.

THE TRIUMPHANT DEATH OF MY DEAR BROTHERS, WOODLOCK AND BARTHOLOMEW.

BUT in the midst of our work, true as we were to each other as brothers and to the principles of the Cross, death's rude hand came among us and made a breach. We were all three labouring for God at Chingford, Essex. The following extract, which at the time was printed as a leaflet, will afford an explanation :—

SUDDEN DEATH OF ONE OF THE "CONVERTED GIPSY BROTHERS" SMITH.

These devoted Christian men had been holding services at Chingford, Essex, since 4th March, 1882, and on Tuesday, 7th March, at the close of their meeting, the second eldest brother, Woodlock, was detained a few minutes behind his brothers in earnest conversation with an anxious soul, and they went on ahead to take train for Stratford, leaving him to make haste after them. Woodlock in the darkness ran with great force against a wooden post in the midst of one of the lanes, and sustained such severe internal injuries that he never rallied, but died in 28 hours. Cornelius, his eldest brother, stayed by him all night, while Bartholomew, the youngest, returned to Stratford to inform their wives and families. On Wednesday morning early Woodlock's wife went to Chingford, and during the day he was removed to his own little home, Cobbold Road, Leytonstone, where he breathed his last early on Thursday, 9th March. Though under terrible suffering he never once lost his consciousness, but to the end testified of redeeming love. He was a large-hearted Christian man, and never happier than when pressing others, in his own simple forceful way, to accept God's gift of salvation, and faithfully to serve the Master he loved so well. He has left a widow, a grown-up son and daughter, and an idiot boy twelve years of age, to mourn his loss.

On Saturday, 11th March, 1882, this worthy Christian man and zealous worker was buried in Leytonstone churchyard. He was followed by his sorrowing relatives, and over fifty of the gipsy community, while four hundred sympathising friends lined the approaches to the church and burying-place. The parish church had a very unusual audience that day, for the gipsy people pressed in with the others, and as the vicar read the burial service hearts were deeply touched and tears freely flowed, and again when the body was committed to the dust, "in sure and certain hope of the resurrection," the wave of hearty response told how solid was that blessed hope of Woodlock. At the grave two or three Christian men addressed the company, testifying to his sterling worth who had just been laid to rest, urging on the unsaved immediate decision for Christ, and on Christians heartier service for the Master. The two surviving brothers spoke very feelingly of the loved one they were severed from, and how much they would feel the missing link in their chain of Gospel testimony. Hymns having been sung with much emotion, prayer was offered, and the company dispersed.

Woodlock Smith was a hale man, only forty-eight years of age. More than twelve years before, his two brothers and he were converted to God, and straightway they began to testify, "Come, see a man which told me all things which ever I did. Is not this the Christ?" And lovingly and earnestly they laboured together from that date. When not called out to Gospel testimony up and down the English counties, they laboured with their own hands. In their services, Woodlock, as a rule, led off with the first address, and afterwards gave out the closing hymn.

On Tuesday evening, at Chingford, he gave out and sang with full heart and soul—

"Sing, oh, sing, of my Redeemer!
With His blood He purchased me!
On the cross He sealed my pardon,
Paid the debt, and made me free!"

About an hour afterwards he met with his accident, and when he was picked up, he said to the helpers, "I have got my death-blow. My work on earth is done, but all's bright above, and I'm going home." He was no ordinary man. In clear incisive Gospel testimony, the blood of Jesus Christ, His finished work on the Cross of Calvary, as alone the ground of the sinners' acceptance with God, and a consequent life of consecration to His service, was the burden of his discourses.

Over the doorway of his cottage home stands this Scripture, "When I see the blood, I will pass over you."

Intensely real in what he said, never did he rise to such a pitch of earnestness as when setting forth, "Ruin by the fall, redemption by the blood of Christ, and regeneration by the Holy Ghost." Within an hour of his departure he turned to his weeping relatives and said, "I am going to heaven, through the blood of the Lamb. Do you love and serve Jesus. Tell the people wherever you go about Him. Be faithful, speak to them about the blood that cleanses." Gathering himself up he then said, "What is this that steals upon my frame? Is it death?" and quickly added—

"If this be death, I soon shall be
From every sin and sorrow free.
I shall the King of Glory see.
All is well."

Who made the difference in this man's life and death from that of an ordinary unconverted gipsy? The Lord Jesus Christ.

Thus was our beloved brother taken from us. We had knelt with him at the Cross, laboured together in the cause of Christ, and we shall live together around His resplendent throne.

Two years after the death of Woodlock, when I had scarcely rallied from that heavy blow, my dear brobrother Bartholomew died. I was quite overcome with the death of Woodlock, and now this terrible blow for the time seemed to unfit me for work, but the precious last hours of Bartholomew will live in memory.

His last few days on earth were spent in Mildmay Cottage Hospital, where he was lovingly tended, and all that human skill could devise under the Divine blessing was done for him, but gradually growing weaker, he pleaded to be carried to his own little cottage home at Leytonstone, to die beside his dear wife and children, and the wish was granted. He only survived the removal about ten hours, but to the last he glorified God in the fires of affliction. A few hours before he passed away he called his family to his bedside and implored each of them to meet him in heaven. His dear wife naturally felt it extremely hard to part with him. He rallied somewhat in his last moments, and said, "There! I was almost gone then. They had come for me." When asked who had come, he replied, "My Saviour." Turning to his wife he said, "You are clinging to me; you will not let me go; and I am sure you do not want me to stay here in all this pain. I must go home, I cannot stay here. I have made it all right for you and the children. God will look after you. I know your difficulty, but He will bring you through." Trying to comfort her I said, "Tell the Lord, Thy will be done." She looked at me, and said, "Oh, it is so hard." I said, "Yes, but the Lord is going to take him to Himself, and it will make it easier for you." We then knelt down. He sat up in the bed with his hands clasped, looking at her, whilst she poured out her soul before the Lord, and told Him her difficulty. God gave her the victory. She said, "I can now say, Thy will be done." She then kissed him once more on earth, and then he clapped his hands and said, "Now I can go, can't I? I am ready to be offered up. The time of my departure is at hand. Lord, let Thy servant depart in peace. Receive my spirit, for Jesus' sake." Bartholomew's soul had fled from its tenement of clay. The bed-chamber was filled with a halo of glory. He was interred in Leytonstone parish churchyard, in the same grave with our dear brother Woodlock, there to await the resurrection morn.

Six months after Bartholomew had passed away God gave to his widow another life, and true to His own promise He has sustained her and her nine children.

A very singular thing happened just before Bartholomew died. He said, "There is another going on a long journey," and he also mentioned the name of one of his married daughters, and twelvemonths to the very day she was laid in her grave, and we trust she has gone to be with Jesus.

Two years before my brother Bartholomew's death God gave me another helper in my dear wife. He knew when He took away my dear brothers that I should feel their loss, and feel unfit to go to meetings alone, so my wife was given me. She had been in the mission work for years, and had been made very useful both in connection with the Christian Missions, in whose meetings she was converted, and also in the Salvation Army. And now, while we write, the Lord is making us a great blessing. Our time is fully spent in the Lord's work, and wherever we go souls are saved and saints are blessed. Jesus Christ found me a poor wandering, neglected, simple gipsy, and brought me into the light, the eternal light of God, and I want to preach Him to my fellow-men as long as I live,

"Happy if with my latest breath
I may but gasp His name;
Preach Him to all, and cry in death,
'Behold, behold the Lamb.'"

THE END.

JOHN HEYWOOD, Excelsior Printing and Bookbinding Works,
Manchester.

www.ingramcontent.com/pod-product-compliance
Lightning Source LLC
LaVergne TN
LVHW080248110826
845148LV00023BA/869

9781535813341